CUSHIONS
& COVERS

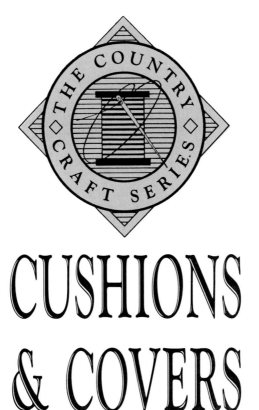

THE COUNTRY CRAFT SERIES

CUSHIONS & COVERS

Jane Bolsover

Bloomsbury Books
London

Previous page: A collection of different shapes of cushions in various weaves, with a double thickness of piping and fringe trims. This combination is an excellent example of how texture and pattern can work well together.

Acknowledgements
Photographs opposite the title page, Introduction and on page 36 provided by Osborne & Little; pages 8, 23, 29 provided by Sanderson; page 30 provided by Dorma.

To Paul.

Published by Harlaxton Publishing Ltd
2 Avenue Road, Grantham, Lincolnshire, NG31 6TA, United Kingdom.
A member of the Weldon International Group of Companies.

First published in 1994

This edition published in 1994 by
Bloomsbury Books
an imprint of
The Godfrey Cave Group
42 Bloomsbury Street, London. WC1B 3QJ
under license from Harlaxton Publishing Ltd.

Publisher: Robin Burgess
Editor: Dulcie Andrews
Illustrator: Sam Denley
Photographer: James Duncan
Typesetting: Sellers, Grantham
Colour separation: G A Graphics, Stamford
Produced in Singapore by Imago

British Library Cataloguing-in-Publication data.
A catalogue record for this book is available from the British Library.
Title: Country Craft Series: Cushions and Covers
ISBN: 1-85471-437-6

CONTENTS

INTRODUCTION

Through this Country Craft series, it is our hope that you will find satisfaction and enjoyment in learning a new skill – in this case, that of making cushions and covers. This book gives you more than inspiration. It provides a basic understanding of the craft and the design skills needed to make beautiful cushions and covers for your home and as gifts for friends. Fortunately, you do not have to be extremely wealthy to enjoy having beautiful fabrics in your home, whether as a table cloth, a throw on the sofa, or as cushions. The art of making soft furnishings is open to everyone willing to learn. *Cushions and Covers* is a great place to start.

Opposite: A wonderful example of using the same fabric in different combinations of blue and cream for cushions, an elaborate wall hanging and as an elegant cover for a straight-backed chair. The piping on the chair seat edge is simple but without it the chair covering would not have the same appeal.

Getting Started

CUSHIONS AND COVERS are versatile soft furnishings that can be used in almost every room of your home. They offer one of the quickest and most economical ways in which to restore worn pieces of furniture and brighten up existing design schemes. Being able to make your own cushions and covers will not only bring you great personal satisfaction, but also give your home that special individual touch. Cushions are one of the simplest fabric accessories to make for your home and because of the small cost involved they are a great starting point for the beginner. Once your have mastered the basic technique there is no limit to the decorative possibilities. The idea of making covers for your furniture may seem daunting and complicated, but covers are just a transition from cushions; most covers are based on the making of a cushion – just with the addition of a skirt.

Cushions have been in existence in some form for centuries. The Chinese and Japanese have used them as their main pieces of furniture since the time of the Ancient Dynasties. The very first cushions, however, were made long before that from rolled up furs or skins. Decorative cushions began to appear in the Greek and Roman civilizations, where they were considered, along with most other types of furnishing, a status symbol. It was not until around the beginning of the 17th century that at last greater numbers of people were able to provide themselves with higher levels of comfort.

Covers, likewise, were developed for the wealthy classes. They were not originally used for decoration but as a practical means of protecting precious upholstery or fabrics from wear and deterioration. During the 19th century covers were widely used, due to the fashion of hair oils for men. The covers became increasingly decorative, left in place for everyday use and removed only for special occasions.

CHOOSING A PROJECT

As this is a book for beginners, we recommend that large-scale coverings such as loose covers for sofas be left to the professional upholsterer. Large volumes of fabric are involved in this type of project and it can become extremely costly should anything go wrong. Here you will find reference to smaller and easier projects, for instance, new seat cushions and arm covers as a disguise for worn areas on sofas. A throw can transform a tired piece of furniture; it is cheap and easy to make and very simple to arrange over the back of the sofa or chair. Quilts and shawls make extremely good throws, as does a large piece of cotton sheeting draped and knotted.

Opposite: Country kitchen chairs are made more comfortable with the addition of seat cushions and small gathered chair skirts.

Various other small-scale items of furniture can easily be given a new look to suit your home; old tables, dining chairs and even desks become smart when covered with fabric. A deep window sill, a wooden bench, wicker furniture and deck chairs are made more comfortable with the addition of soft cushions. You may like to make large square cushions as extra floor seating. Piled one on top of the other in a corner, these can look most attractive.

The bedroom is the perfect place for decorative, imaginative cushions. Be creative; your cushions can be frilled, pleated or trimmed with a piece of contrasting piping. Bring colour and texture to your design by adding fabric flowers, using a fabric that is already quilted or working with squares of patchwork. Ribbon trims, extravagant tassels and bright cord around the edges provide important finishing touches. The choice of ideas is endless but it is important to be quite clear about the style you want for your home before you begin.

FINDING YOUR STYLE

Magazines and illustrated home decorating books are great sources of inspiration. Invest in a scrap book and collect photographs, fabric cuttings, pieces of wallpaper and anything visual which appeals to you and, before long, you will find that you are drawn to a particular theme, style and colour mix. Use this source material to help create the look which most suits your life-style. There are no rules to follow when decorating but you may like to take into consideration the period and style of your property and decorate it appropriately. Use reference books to help you develop a feel for the style of the era.

Alternatively, the shape of your furniture can be a determining factor. Straight or angular pieces look good with smart, smooth covering; rounded furniture is more suited to a softer look, perhaps with pleats, frills and bows. It is most important to take your time to decide on the style you want to have around you.

MOOD AND COLOUR

Few people have the opportunity to decorate their homes from scratch and a large piece of existing furniture, a carpet or curtains can be the initial inspiration for a theme. Great care must be taken when choosing your colour scheme, as this will play a large part in creating the right mood for your room. Yellow, golden and coral tones present a warm and welcoming feel, whereas blue, grey and pale neutral shades produce a cooler atmosphere. Deeper shades will create a cosy mood but can make rooms seems smaller. White and pale tones give a clean and fresh feeling and make a room seem larger but, like shades of blue, can give a cool impression, so are best used in sunny, hot rooms. Look through paint charts to get a good idea of which shades work well together. By using strong contrasts you can create a lively atmosphere; subtle combinations, which create a calmer mood, need to be thought about carefully or the end result can be bland and visually boring.

PATTERN AND TEXTURE

An attractive printed fabric is also a good basis for a scheme. There is a wide variety available, from large and small florals to modern abstract and geometric designs. An hour spent in the fabric store will bring your likes and dislikes into focus.

Different patterns can be mixed success-fully by linking designs through common shades; for instance, using deep and pale pink together. Following this method, you can mix stripes and checks, tying them to the original scheme. It is best to keep schemes simple to begin with, becoming more adventurous as you feel more confident.

Texture is often thought to be less important that shade and pattern, but it is the texture that adds life to a fabric and creates its main appeal. The rich pile on velvet gives a depth to the red, yellow, green or gold, while the crispness of linen gives a smooth natural finish to the cushion or cover. The sheen on a piece of natural silk tells us this is a luxurious piece of fabric and should be treated in a magnificent manner. These textural differ-ences are especially important in a mono-chromatic or neutral scheme, but it is also important to remember texture when you are looking at fabrics that are colourful and patterned.

The most successful schemes will be a combination of fabrics with colour, pattern and texture in harmony. As an exercise, collect samples of the fabrics you like. These samples should not be equal in size but proportional to their finished use; for instance, a cutting representing the main area of a cushion will need to be larger than one for the trim.

Look at them in the room in which they are going to be situated in both natural and artificial lighting. Swap them or replace them until you are happy with the end result. Time spent at this stage will ensure you are not disappointed with the end result.

TOOLS AND MATERIALS

YOU WILL FIND cushions and covers much easier and more enjoyable to sew if you use the correct tools and materials but this does not mean you have to rush out and spend a fortune. No more specialized equipment is required than you would need for home dressmaking. Careful thought is required, however, when choosing your materials to avoid disappointment with the result.

FABRICS

Almost any fabric can be used for a cover from heavy tapestry to delicate cottons and lace but when choosing materials for your projects, one of the most important elements to consider is the wear and tear the final article will receive. Seat cushions and covers in busy living areas will obviously get a lot of wear, therefore they need to be made from durable fabrics with a firm weave; velvet, brocade, corduroy, heavy-weight cotton, linen or union (a mixture of cotton and linen) are all suitable. Leave chintz and cotton sateen fabrics for bedroom areas or occasional chairs. Scatter cushions are not exposed to the same amount of wear, so you can use any type of fabric including dress materials. Fabrics made from natural fibres, for example, cotton, linen, wool and silk, are more suitable for home furnishings, as synthetics may collect static electricity, and

so attract dirt.

When buying your fabric, you will need to allow extra if you have chosen a printed design and want to place a motif centrally on each piece. It may also be necessary for you to match the design across seams, especially on table cloths and throws. A striped fabric can be used running in different directions on gussets and edgings; contrasting fabrics, mixed on one cover, can look very exciting.

To work out exactly how much fabric you will need to buy, draw out your pattern pieces and arrange them into the fabric width. Before you start to cut out, check for any fabric faults as most companies will not exchange cloth once you have cut into it. Faults are sometimes marked with a tag on the selvedge.

The selvedge is the firmly woven edge running down both sides of the fabric. On a printed cloth there may be information about the care of the fabric down the edges. When cutting out you should always trim off the selvedge, and make sure that your pieces are cut straight and square, with one side parallel to the selvedge wherever possible.

CUSHION PADS

Although you can make your own cushion pads, at this stage it is best to buy the pre-formed variety available from most large

Opposite: The front cushion has been cleverly coordinated to the others by using simple applique and quilting techniques. The result is a group of beautiful cushions.

13

Above: Preformed cushion pads in a variety of shapes can be purchased from most large department stores.

department stores, craft and furnishing fabric shops. When choosing a pad, do not only consider the shape and size but also what type of filling the pad contains, as this could effect its end use. Once you have mastered the art of making cushions it will be possible for you to make your own individually shaped pads. Make a cover to the shape and size you require in a firmly woven fabric, following the basic slip stitch method (p.19), and stuff it with your chosen filling.

Down and feather – Down is the softest cushion filling and also the most expensive, therefore it is often mixed with feathers to reduce the price. Feather pads can be firmly stuffed (making them suitable for deep-seat cushions) or more softly filled (for scatter cushions and pillows). Both types are extremely comfortable and can be 'reshaped' by plumping up time after time.

Polyester and acrylic wadding (batting) – Pads with this filling are less expensive and have the advantage of being completely washable, making them particularly suitable for children's areas and outdoors. They are not as soft as feather pads and tend to have an over-stuffed look that can permanently flatten with prolonged use.

Foam chips – This is the cheapest form of filling and, although pads made with these have the advantage of being washable, they have a springy feel and, unless the chips are firmly packed, they will tend to look lumpy.

Foam blocks – Foam is available in various

Above: A selection of the basic items. Having the correct equipment makes sewing a lot easier and much more enjoyable.

qualities and thicknesses and is ideal for indoor and out-door deep-seat cushions. The foam is cut to your required shape either by the supplier or at home, using a Stanley knife. Once the pad has been cut it will not lose its original shape; the only downfall is that, in time, it will begin to deteriorate and crumble. Therefore, you will need to cover your pad with an inner lining before making your outer cover. This type of pad can be given a softer look by sticking a layer of polyester wadding (batting) to the top and bottom flat surfaces before covering it with your liner.

Polystyrene balls – This is the filling you find in bean bags. It is very cheap, with a firm and springy feel and the ability to flow freely around the inside of the cushion. It is this quality that makes it particularly suitable for floor cushions, as the balls can mould themselves around the body of whoever is sitting on the cushion and adjust for comfort as the sitter moves.

Safety factors – Remember always to look for flame-retardent finishes when you are choosing your pad. Both foam and poly-styrene are highly inflammable materials that give off toxic fumes if they catch fire.

EQUIPMENT

Sewing machine – A simple, straight-stitch machine or, preferably, one that also does zigzag stitch, is all that is required for the basic sewing of cushions and covers. Since this is the most expensive piece of equipment you will need, go along to a large shop or store and try out as many models as possible before making your selection. Some machines offer lots of fancy stitches but, unless you plan to use them on a regular basis for decoration, it will not be worth the investment. One accessory which is very helpful is the zipper foot, which enables you to sew zips in place and attach piping. Read the manual carefully to get to know how your machine works before you start to sew.

Steam iron – This is used to iron out fabric creases and to press seams flat as they are sewn for a professional finish. Both heat and steam are necessary for good pressing; if you do not own a steam iron, use a damp muslin cloth between your fabric and the iron. Make sure that your iron has a clean sole plate and is in good working order – especially the thermostat controlling the temperature. To be safe, always test your iron heat on a spare piece of your fabric before starting to press.

Machine needles – There are various sizes of needle available for use with different weights of fabric. Make sure you choose one which is the correct size and type for your machine.

Hand-sewing needles – There are various types and sizes available. For general-purpose sewing sharps are the most useful. An upholstery needle can be handy for sewing into cushioned surfaces; they are curved in shape and, therefore, make the attaching of braid and cord decorations to a finished article much easier.

Pins – Use stainless steel pins as they do not rust and can be collected with a magnet. Store them in a pin cushion so that the ends do not become bent and blunt. Dressmaker's pins, available in two lengths, are suitable for most fabrics but, if you are working with delicate materials, use lace pins which are extra fine.

Thread – Polyester thread is the best all-round choice for both hand- and machine-sewing. Being synthetic, it is strong, shrink resistant and will stretch without snapping. Mercerized cotton is best left for woven cotton, linen and rayon fabrics, as it has no give and will break easily under strain. Always choose a thread one shade darker than your fabric or, if you are using a printed fabric, match it to the main colour.

Scissors and shears – Use bent-handled dressmaker's shears for cutting fabric. They have angled blades which allow the fabric to lie flat as you cut, making cutting out much more accurate. A pair of light trimmers are good for trimming and clipping seams. Keep embroidery scissors for unpicking and trimming threads. Pinking shears are useful if your sewing machine does not do zigzag stitch. They have zigzag blades which are excellent for neatening seams and raw edges.

Tailor's chalk – This is used to mark out your pattern pieces on to fabric ready for cutting out. Wax markers are also available for this job but they can leave marks on your finished article that are hard to remove.

Tape measure – An essential piece of kit for most measuring jobs, the best type of tape measures have metal ends and are made from plastic or plastic-coated material which will not stretch or tear. It is also less frustrating if your tape is reversible, enabling you to read the numbers from both sides and ends.

Ruler – A long ruler or metre stick is useful for measuring and drawing long, straight lines on to fabric or paper when cutting out or making a pattern.

Set square – These are triangular in shape

Above: These old deck chairs have been given a face lift with a lick of paint and new covers. Square cushions have been added for extra comfort and these are held in place with ties, Velcro or snap fasteners to the top rail.

with a true right angle, which will help you to find the bias grain on a fabric. Usually made from clear plastic, some have measurements along their edges and can be used like a ruler.

Thimble – These are worn on your middle finger for protection when hand sewing. They can be quite uncomfortable, so make sure you choose one that really fits. Thimbles are especially useful when working on thicker types of fabrics.

Bodkin – These come in handy for threading cord or elastic through narrow casings. They look rather like large blunt needles, with either an eye or a slit through which to thread your cord.

Knitting needle – A spare medium-sized needle is useful for poking out corners and for turning ties through to the right side after machining.

STARTING WORK

THE STEP-BY-STEP instructions that follow show you in easy stages how to make basic covers for cushions, chairs, tables and beds. If you are a beginner, it is best to start with one of these simple shapes but, once you feel more adept at the craft, you can adapt the principles to make any shape of cover you require.

The sewing techniques used in making these covers, are explained more fully in the next chapter 'Techniques of the Craft'.

WORK SPACE

Before you start to sew, decide on a suitable working area. The ideal situation is a room permanently set up with your equipment and with adequate storage space for your materials but, of course, not everyone has the space available. Wherever you choose, be it the dining room, kitchen, or a spare bedroom, it is essential that you have sufficient space, a strong table and good lighting.

GENERAL POINTS – PLEASE NOTE

Use a 15mm (⅝ inch) seam allowance throughout these instructions. Sew all seams with the right sides of the fabric facing, unless otherwise stated, and neaten all raw edges for a professional finish.

SQUARE CUSHIONS

Square and rectangular cushions are the most popular, ranging from small scatter cushions to the very large floor type. Their covers are easy to make, with a choice of methods depending on the sort of opening and fastening you prefer.

Basic square cushion pattern

Measure both the width and the length of your cushion pad across the centre (this will show you if your pad is square or a rectangle). On a piece of paper, draw out your shape to these dimensions, then add the seam allowance to all sides to complete your pattern.

Slip stitch method

1. Using your pattern, cut out two pieces of fabric.
2. Seam (p.32) the two fabric pieces together, leaving a large opening along one side (Fig.1).
3. Turn the cover right-side out. Fold the seam allowance to the inside along both raw opening edges and press flat.
4. Insert the cushion pad through the opening, pushing it well into the corners.
5. Slip stitch (p.31) the pressed edges together.

This method can be adapted to make duvet covers. Simply attach press studs (snap fasteners), or nylon fastener tape (p.34) to the opening edges before turning your cover through to the right side.

Opposite: Here is a wonderful example of mixing a printed fabric with checks and stripes to create a successful colour scheme.

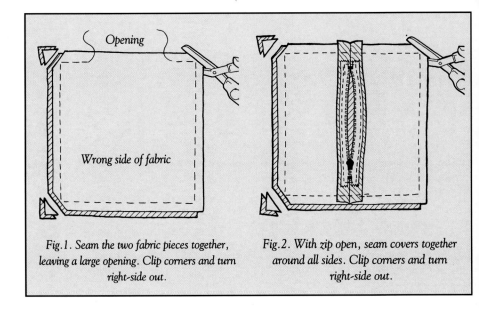

Fig.1. Seam the two fabric pieces together, leaving a large opening. Clip corners and turn right-side out.

Fig.2. With zip open, seam covers together around all sides. Clip corners and turn right-side out.

Zipped method

1. Make a pattern for your front cover following the basic square pattern instructions above. For the back cover, draw a second piece the same size; fold and cut this piece exactly in half. Discard one portion and add a seam allowance to the cut edge of the remaining piece. This will form your centre back seam.

2. Using your pattern, cut out one front cover and two back covers in fabric.

3. Insert a zip into the centre back seam.

4. With the zip open, seam (p.32) the front and back covers together around all four sides (Fig.2). Turn the cover through to the right side and press flat.

Pillowcase method

1. Make a front and back pattern following the basic square instructions. Draw a flap pattern piece, the width of the cushion cover x 10cm (4 inches) deep, remember to add a seam allowance to all sides.

2. Using your pattern, cut out one front cover, one back cover and one flap piece in fabric.

3. Neaten one edge of the front cover and one long edge of the flap with a 6mm (¼ inch) double turned hem (p.33).

4. Seam (p.32) the remaining long raw edge of the flap to one edge of the back cover. Press seam flat.

5. Place the front cover on top of the back cover, with the flap out straight. Seam the three remaining un-hemmed edges together, starting and finishing at front cover hem edge.

6. Fold the flap on to the wrong side of the front cover and sew the side edges in place through all fabric layers (Fig.3). Turn the cover right-side out and press flat. Insert

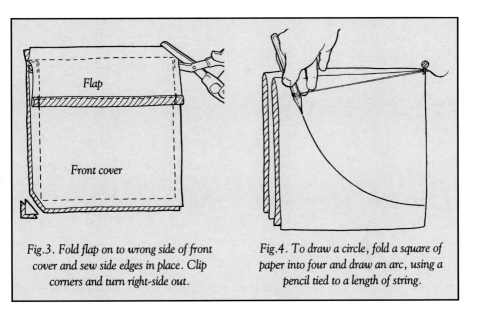

Fig.3. Fold flap on to wrong side of front cover and sew side edges in place. Clip corners and turn right-side out.

Fig.4. To draw a circle, fold a square of paper into four and draw an arc, using a pencil tied to a length of string.

the pad into the cover under the flap.

This method can be used to make pillow-cases for your bed, but you may wish to allow for a deeper hem on the front cover.

ROUND CUSHIONS

Once you have made your pattern, round cushions are worked in a similar way to the square covers.

Basic round pattern

Measure the diameter of your cushion pad and divide it by two to find your radius. It is best to take 2.5cm (1 inch) away from your radius measurement at this stage, to ensure that your final cushion will look well filled out (this instruction applies only to round cushions and not to any of the other uses for this pattern mentioned later on in the chapter). Cut a square of paper larger than the diameter of your pad and fold it into four.

Tie a piece of string to a pencil and, starting at the pencil point, measure the radius distance along the string and push a drawing pin through the string at this position. Place the folded paper on a piece of board or similar surface and push the drawing pin in at the folded corner. Keeping the string taut, use it like a pair of compasses to draw your arc (Fig.4). Add the seam allowance to the outer edge and cut out the pattern whilst the paper is still folded.

Slip stitch method

Using the basic round pattern instructions, make a cover following the square cushions slip stitch method (above).

Zipped method

Using the basic round pattern instructions, make a cover following the square cushions zipped method (above).

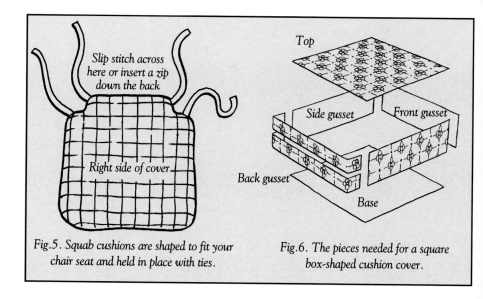

Fig.5. Squab cushions are shaped to fit your chair seat and held in place with ties.

Fig.6. The pieces needed for a square box-shaped cushion cover.

SQUAB CUSHIONS

These cushions are similar to square and round cushions in that they comprise of two sections, a top and a base. The difference is that they are shaped to fit chair seats and held in place either with four ties at the leg positions or two at the back uprights (Fig.5). You may have to make your own cushion pad to fit your seat; this is easy to do by making a pattern as outlined below, omitting the ties and consulting p.14 for filling suggestions.

Basic squab method

1. Lay a sheet of tracing paper on top of your seat and trace around the shape. Mark the position of the legs or the back uprights, depending on where you attach your ties. Add the seam allowance to the outer edge. Fold your tracing in half and cut out on the double to ensure an even shape.

2. The cover can be made by following either the slip stitch, or the zipped methods

shown for the square cushion covers (p.20), but remember to attach your ties at the correct position (see p.35 for the tie make-up or use ribbon or braid), before sewing the top and bottom covers togeter.

BOX CUSHION COVER

These covers are for deeper cushions, as found on a sofa, window seat or wicker chair. They consist of a top and base section which are joined together with a side gusset. Boxed cushions can be square, round or shaped to fit the exact shape of your seat. They need large openings to make the insertion of the pad as easy as possible.

Square box shape

1. Draw a pattern for the top and base sections following the basic square cushion pattern (p.19). You will also need three gusset pieces. The front section is the same width as the pad x the depth, the back

*Opposite: A squab cushion has been made to fit the seat of this wooden settle
and carefully trimmed with fabric covered piping and buttons.*

section is the width of the pad plus 10cm (4 inches), this allows the opening to fall around to the sides x half the depth of the pad and, finally, the side section is the length of the side, minus 5cm (2 inches) x the depth of the pad (Fig.6). Remember to add the seam allowances to all sides of each pattern piece.

2. Using your pattern, cut out one top, one base, one front gusset, two back gussets and two side gussets in fabric.

3. Insert a zip (p.20) between the long edges of the back gusset pieces.

4. Seam (p.32) the short ends of the side gussets to the front and joined back gussets to form a circle. Place your gusset around your pad to check the fit.

5. Pin the top section to one edge of your gusset, matching the front corners to the front seams and seam in place.

6. Open your zip, then pin and seam the base section to the remaining raw edge of the gusset. Turn the cover right-side out and press flat.

Round box shape

1. Draw a top and base pattern following the basic round cushion pattern (p.21). You will also need two gusset pieces. The front gusset is half of the circumference of your top cover x the depth of your pad. The back gusset is the same length as the front, but only half the depth of the pad.

2. Using your pattern, cut out one top, one base, one front gusset and two back gussets in fabric.

3. Insert zip and seam gussets following steps 3 and 4 of the square cushion box method (above).

4. Seam (p.32) the top piece to one edge of the gusset, open the zip and seam the base

to the other edge. Turn the cover to the right side and press.

Individual box shapes

The easiest way to make a pattern for the top and base sections of a shaped pad is to lay your pad on to a large sheet of paper and carefully draw around the outer edge. You will need to make gusset pieces to fit the outer edge x the depth of your pad. Try to join your gusset pieces so that they will match up to any front corners on your pad and allow for a large opening on your back gusset pieces. Remember to add the seam allowances to all pieces and make the cover following one, or a combination of the above methods, depending on the shape of your pad.

BOLSTER CUSHIONS

A bolster cushion is really an elongated box cushion, where the gusset has increased in depth to form the main area of the cushion and the top and base reduced to form small circular ends. There are three basic methods for covering a bolster (Fig.7).

Flat end method

1. Measure the length, circumference and diameter of the bolster pad. Draw out your main pattern, the length x the circumference, and add your seam allowance to all sides. For your end piece, divide the diameter by two to find the radius. Follow the basic round pattern instructions (p.21).

2. Using the pattern, cut one main piece and two end pieces in fabric.

3. Fold the main cover in half along its length and insert a zip (p.20) between the long sides.

4. Complete the cover following step 4 of the round box shape (opposite).

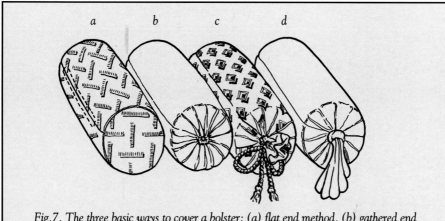

Fig.7. *The three basic ways to cover a bolster: (a) flat end method, (b) gathered end method, (c) cracker method, tied and (d) cracker method, knotted.*

Gathered end method

1. Measure the length, circumference and diameter of the bolster pad. Draw out a pattern, the length of the pad plus the diameter x the circumference. Add the seam allowance to all sides.
2. Using the pattern, cut out one piece in fabric.
3. Fold the cover in half lengthways and seam (p.32) the long sides together to form a tube. Press the seam flat and turn the cover right-side out.
4. Stitch a 15mm (⅝ inch) deep, single turned hem (p.33) on both raw ends of the cover. Insert the pad centrally along the cover.
5. Run a row of hand-sewn gathering stitches (p.31) around the hems at each end of the cover. Pull the gathers up tightly into a circle, so the cover moulds around the ends of the pad.

Cracker method

This cover is made following the gathered end method, but it is cut much longer than the length of your pad plus the diameter. The ends on this style are gathered together in your hands and tied in place with ribbon or cord to create the cracker effect. The extra length required for this cover depends on the effect you wish to create. The ends, after tying, can be as short as 5cm (2 inches) or they can be left long and flowing. If you are using a very soft fabric, it is even possible to knot the ends to form your cracker shape.

CHAIR ARM COVERS

These are cheap, very simple to make and an ideal way to cover up worn arm areas on sofas and armchairs.

Basic arm cover method

1. Remove the seat cushions from your sofa or chair.
2. Place a sheet of tracing paper up to the front of the arm. Carefully trace around the arm shape, marking the seat position on

Fig.8. Seam the top cover to outer edge of front piece, clip seams and press. Neaten the remaining raw edges with double turned hems.

the inner edge of the arm.

3. Square off the base of your pattern at the seat position using a set square (see page 16).

4. Measure around the outer edge of your pattern from one base corner to the other. Measure the length along the sofa arm to where you want the cover to finish. Draw an oblong to these dimensions for your top cover. Add the seam allowance to all sides on both pattern pieces.

5. Using your pattern, cut out one front and one top cover in fabric for each arm (remember to turn your front pattern piece over when cutting your second arm).

6. Seam (p.32) one long edge of the top cover to the outer edge of the front piece, starting and finishing at the base corners; press flat.

7. Neaten the remaining raw edges with a 6mm (¼ inch) deep, double turned hem (p.33) (Fig.8).

TABLE CLOTHS

Table cloths are not only a protective layer but they can also be a permanent decorative feature for your room.

Square or rectangular draped cloth method

1. Measure the length and width of your table and decide on the overhang you require and the depth of your hem. Double the overhang and hem measurement and add this figure to each of the table-top dimensions.

2. The hem depth will depend on the type of finish you desire. It can be a simple narrow hem, or a deeper one with mitred corners (p.33). You may choose to have a scalloped edge or, perhaps, add a frill (see p.39).

3. You may have to join fabric widths to obtain the right size of cloth. Never make a join down the centre of your table cloth, simply split your extra width in half and seam it to each side of your main fabric piece. Remember, if you need to join fabric widths always to add the extra seam allowances before cutting out your pieces.

Circular draped cloth method

1. Measure the diameter of your table top, decide on the overhang you require and the depth of your hem. To find your cloth diameter, double the overhang measurement plus the hem and add this figure to the table-top diameter.

2. Hems should be kept as small as possible on a circular cloth. Choose between a narrow single or double hem (p.33) or, alternatively, bind the edge (p.37). For a feminine touch, you could make a pretty scalloped or frilled edging.

3. Join fabric widths if necessary to obtain your size, as shown in step 3 of the square draped cloth (above).

Above: A Collection of square and rectangular cushions is enhanced with coordinating fringing and cord trims. The ends of the bolster are defined with piping set into seams.

4. To draw your circular shape, find the radius of your cloth by dividing the diameter by two. Follow the instructions for the basic round cushion pattern (p.21) but draw your shape directly on to the wrong side of your fabric.

Fitted cloth method

The simplest form of fitted cloth is made from two main pieces; a top which is cut to fit the surface of your table and a separate skirt that forms the overhang. Fitted cloths can also be made in three pieces, with a gusset strip between the top and skirt sections. The gusset is attached to the top section in the same way as for a box cushion, with all the gussets cut the same depth – usually between 5cm (2 inches) and 10cm (4 inches) and their joining seams placed at each corner on a square cloth. The skirt is then seamed to the lower edge of the gusset.

The skirt section for either style can be straight, pleated, or gathered (Fig.9). Once again, the choice of hems depends entirely on the finish you desire.

The fitted cloth method it is easy to scale up in size to make a valance for your bed. Always remember to add seam allowances to all pieces, otherwise your cloth or valance will not fit.

THROWS

Throws are traditionally used over beds but, as we suggested in the previous chapter, they are excellent for covering up worn sofas. The simplest form of throw is made like a large square or rectangular draped cloth but they are much nicer if you line them with a matching or contrasting fabric.

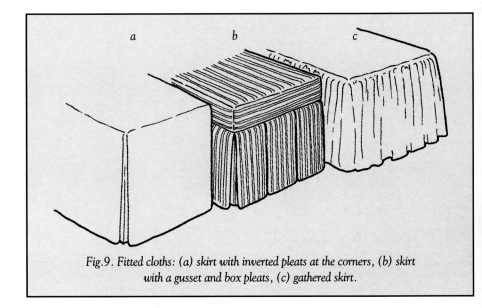

Fig.9. Fitted cloths: (a) skirt with inverted pleats at the corners, (b) skirt with a gusset and box pleats, (c) gathered skirt.

Lined throw method

The top and lining are both made in the same way and are cut equal in size.

1. Measure the length and width of your bed with the bedding and pillows in place, allowing extra length for tucking your throw behind the pillows. Follow steps 1 and 3 of the square or rectangular draped cloth but allow for a normal seam allowance only on the side edges.

2. To complete your throw, turn to steps 2, 3 and 5 of the square cushion slip stitch method (p.19).

Bound edge method

Throws can also be finished with a bound edge. Here the seam allowance is not required on the outer edges of your throw. Instead you will need to round off the corners, using a plate as a template, to make it easier to apply your binding.

1. Place the top cover on top of the lining with wrong sides facing.

2. Tack the layers together around the outer edge and apply the binding strip (p.37).

Opposite: A scalloped, flat border has been set into the side seams of this duvet cover and pillowcase to echo the Medieval style of the bed drapes.

TECHNIQUES OF THE CRAFT

IN THIS chapter you will find instructions for the basic sewing techniques required to make cushions and covers. Choose a simple project to begin with where you can practise these techniques before you progress on to a more ambitious task.

HAND SEWN STITCHES

These are worked for a right-handed person; reverse directions if you are left handed.

Hemming stitch

This stitch is used to secure a hem in place when you do not want a line of machining showing on the right side. It is worked from right to left, over the hem edges. Fasten your thread to the inside of the hem. Hold your needle diagonally and move 9mm (⅜ inch) to the left. Pick up one or two threads from your main fabric and pass the needle through the top of the hem edge. Draw the thread right through to form a slanted stitch.

Overcasting stitch

Use this stitch to neaten the raw edges of fabric to stop them fraying. It can be worked from either the left or the right. Fasten your thread to the inside of the hem by bringing the needle through from the back to the front. Draw the thread over the raw edge and then pass the needle through from the back to the front once again, forming a diagonal stitch. Try to keep your stitches evenly spaced

and of an equal depth.

Running stitch (Gathering stitch)

This is a small, evenly spaced stitch suitable for gathering. It is worked from right to left, by weaving the needle in and out of the fabric several times before pulling the thread through. Work two parallel rows of stitching, approximately 6mm (¼ inch) apart, leaving the threads loose at one end. Keep hold of the threads between your finger and thumb, then carefully move the fabric along the stitches with your other hand until you have the desired gathered effect. Fasten off the thread ends with a knot.

Slip stitch

Worked from right to left, this stitch is used to join two folded edges together invisibly. Attach your thread and bring your needle out through the lower folded edge. For the first and each following stitch, pass the needle directly up or down into the opposite folded edge and slip the needle along the hem for 6mm (¼ inch). Bring the needle out and draw the thread through. Continue along the opening, drawing the edges together.

Tacking stitch (Basting stitch)

These are temporary stitches used to hold layers of fabric in position ready for sewing. They are worked in the same manner as running stitches but are longer, so they can easily be removed after machining.

Opposite: This collection of cushions shows some of the many ways in which the basic shaped covers can be enhanced with trims and surface decorations.

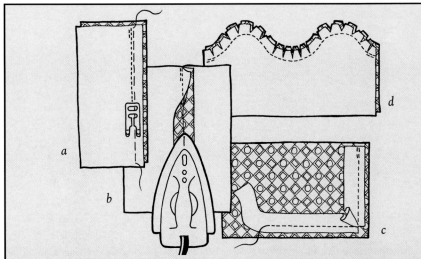

Fig.10. Seams. (a) Place your two pieces together, with right sides facing and raw edges level. Pin, tack and machine 15mm (⅝ inch) in from the raw edge. (b) Remove tacking (basting) stitches and press flat. (c) To apply a straight strip to a corner edge, snip into the seam allowance to allow the strip to bend. (d) Clip curved seams, to ensure a smooth shape when turned to the right side.

SEAMS

Basic method

The simple flat or open seam is most suitable for constructing cushions and covers. It is worked by placing your two pieces of fabric together, with the right sides facing and raw edges level. The edges are then pinned and tacked (basted) just inside your seam line. Using a straight stitch on your machine, sew 15mm (⅝ inch) in from the raw edges, reversing at each end to secure (Fig.10a). Remove tacking (basting) stitches and press the seam allowances open (Fig.10b).

Seaming corners

To seam two flat pieces neatly together around a corner, machine up to the corner stopping 15mm (⅝ inch) before the edge. Make sure your needle is down through the fabric, then lift the machine foot and turn the pieces around, so that the new edge is parallel to the foot. Continue your seam as before. To finish, snip away the seam allowance diagonally close to the point, to reduce bulk, before turning your item through to the right side, carefully pushing out the corners with a knitting needle.

To apply a straight strip, for example, a gusset or piping, to a corner edge, work with your strip on top and start half way along a straight side. Pin and tack (baste) the strip in place, stopping 15mm (⅝ inch) from the corner. Make a snip into the seam allowance on the strip at this point, to allow it to bend around the corner, then continue to pin and tack down the new edge (Fig.10c). Machine and finish as shown for the flat corner.

Seaming curves

After seaming, curved edges need to be clipped to allow for a smooth shape when turned to the right side and pressed. If your seam is convex or outwardly curved, as on a round cushion, you will need to cut small V-shaped notches, at regular intervals, out of the seam allowance. On the other hand, if your seam is concave or inwardly curved, then you need only make straight snips into the seam allowance (Fig.10d).

Neatening seams

Seam allowances need to be neatened to stop them from fraying. Neat seams also give your cushions and covers a professional look. There are three main ways to neaten the raw edges of your seams. If your sewing machine does a zigzag stitch, then set it to a medium size and sew over the edges. The alternatives are hand overcasting stitch (p.31) or, if your fabric does not fray too badly, you can sew a straight stitch row about 6mm (¼ inch) in from the raw edge and then trim close to it with pinking shears.

Plain straight seams should be neatened after pressing but it is best to neaten curved seams before seaming together, as their turnings need to be clipped before pressing.

HEMS

Single turned hem

Neaten the raw edge then simply press up the required hem depth on to the wrong side of the fabric. Machine stitch it in place close to the neatened edge, or use a hand hemming stitch (p. 31).

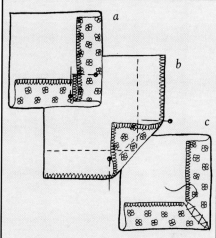

Fig.11. Mitred corners for a single hem. (a) Using pins, mark the position where the neatened edges cross. (b) Unfold hems and press over corner between pins. (c) Re-fold hems to form a mitre and slip stitch edges together.

Double turned hem

The raw edge on this hem does not have to be neatened as it is enclosed within the hem fold. Press the required hem depth on to the wrong side of the fabric, then fold over the pressed hem width once again, so that the raw edge lies inside at the base of the hem. Pin and either machine stitch close to the top folded edge or hand stitch in place.

Mitring corners

It is necessary to mitre corners when your hem is deeper then 12mm (½ inch).

If you are making a single turned hem, neaten and press all the edges to the depth required. At one corner, mark the neatened edges of each hem with pins where they cross

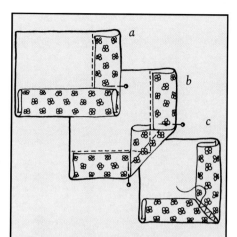

Fig.12. Mitred corner for a double hem.
(a) Using a pin, mark on the single fold
where the double fold touches it. Repeat
with the other side. (b) Unfold both
hems to a single folds, and press over
corner between pins. (c) Re-fold hems to
form mitre and slip stitch edges together.

(Fig.11a). Unfold the hems and press the corner over diagonally between the pins (Fig.11b). Trim away the corner to reduce bulk, leaving a 15mm (⅝ inch) seam allowance. Re-fold the hem sides to form the mitre and slip stitch (p.31) the folded edges together (Fig.11c). Repeat on all corners then sew hems in place as described above.

For a double turned hem, press all the edges to the depth required. Working at one corner unfold one side to a single hem and mark with a pin on the single fold where the double fold crosses it (Fig.12a). Repeat with the other side. Unfold both sides to a single hem and press over the corner diagonally between the pins (Fig.12b). Continue as for

the single hem, only you will be working with two layers of fabric (Fig.12c). Repeat on all the corners and sew in place as shown above.

FASTENINGS
Zips

Various weights and lengths of zips are available in a large range of colours with either nylon or metal teeth. Choose a lightweight zip for scatter cushions and a heavy-duty one for deep seat cushions where it is likely to receive more strain. The length of your zip needs to be approximately 10cm (4 inches) shorter than the seam in which it is to be inserted.

To insert a zip, seam your two pieces together at each end of the zip opening and reverse to secure your stitching. With your machine set to its largest stitch, tack (baste) the zip opening together; do not reverse at the ends. Press the seam open. Working on the wrong side, place your zip centrally face down over the tacked (basted) opening. Pin and hand-tack (baste) it in place through all layers. Then working from the right side and using the zipper foot on your machine, top stitch the zip in place 6mm (¼ inch) each side of the seam line, stitching across the top and base of the zip at the same time. To finish, unpick the machine- and hand-tacking (basting) stitches.

Press-stud (Snap fastener) tape

Press studs (snap fasteners) are made of two parts that clip together. Both metal and plastic studs (snaps) can be bought ready attached, evenly spaced, to a webbing tape. This tape provides a quick and easy method of fastening. It is simple to apply on a square cover made by the slip stitched method, by sewing a piece to each side of the opening.

After pressing the seam allowances to the wrong side on one side of the opening, place a piece of the tape over the turnings, with one edge lined up with the fold. Turn under the raw ends of the tape, then pin, tack (baste) and machine in place around all edges. Repeat on the other side of the opening, making sure that the studs (snaps) line up for fastening.

Nylon tape fastener

Commonly known as Velcro, this tape is also made of two sections; one has a looped surface and one a hooked. When pressed together, the surfaces stick until they are pulled apart. This tape is completely washable and is therefore a suitable fastening for covers that need to be laundered frequently. It is applied in the same manner as the press-stud (snap fastener) tape above.

Buttons

These can be used to fasten covers made by the pillowcase method. You will need to allow a deeper double turned hem on your top cover so that you can sew evenly-spaced button holes, using your machine. Sew buttons to the flap to correspond, reinforcing each button position with a square of interfacing before attaching your buttons.

Ties

These are used to fasten squab cushions to chairs or to fasten the opening on a cover made following the pillowcase method. The ties can be narrow in width or wide, forming large bows. Narrow ties under 18mm (¾ inch) in width are made by cutting a fabric strip 48cm (19 inches) long x four times your finished width for each tie. Press one short end 9mm (⅜ inch) to the wrong side, then press the long raw edges to the wrong side, so they meet down the centre. Fold the strip in half with wrong sides facing and the pressed edges level. Starting at the short raw end, machine the pressed edges together, reversing to secure your stitching at the beginning and end.

For ties over 2.5cm (1 inch) wide, cut a strip 48cm (19 inches) long x twice the finished width, and add a 9mm (⅜ inch) seam allowance on all sides. With right sides of fabric facing, fold the tie in half length-ways and seam the long edges and one short end together. Turn through to the right side and press flat.

The raw ends of the ties can be sandwiched between the seam on a squab cushion, or a 9mm (⅜ inch) hem can be pressed under, so that the end can be stitched to the outside of your cover with a row of boxed (square shaped) machining.

FINISHING TECHNIQUES

THERE ARE infinite combinations of decorative possibilities that you can use on any of the basic covers we have described in the previous chapters. The quickest and easiest way to embellish your covers is with the addition of an edging, whether purchased from one of the fabulous ranges available or made by yourself. Do not forget that cushions can be turned into real masterpieces, when you use them to display a beautiful piece of needlepoint, embroidery or perhaps some precious souvenir.

HAND MADE EDGINGS
Binding

The raw edges of your covers can be neatened and enhanced with the application of a binding. For straight edges, ribbon or braid make ideal binding; for curved edges you will need to use bias binding, which is specially cut on the bias of a fabric to enable it to be bent around curves. Ready-made bias binding can be purchased in a variety of colours and widths, or you can make your own matching trim (see below). To apply binding, neaten the ends first by pressing a small hem to the wrong side, press it in half lengthways with long edges level and raw edges inside, then sandwich the fabric between the binding. Pin, tack (baste) and top stitch the long edges in place through all fabric layers.

How to make bias binding

To cut a bias strip, find the bias grain on your fabric by laying a set square on to the fabric with one edge level with the selvedge. The diagonal edge of your set square will now be running along the bias grain. Place your long ruler or metre stick up to the diagonal edge and draw a straight line across your fabric. Draw a second line parallel to the first, forming a strip four times wider than your finished binding measurement. Repeat this to obtain your correct binding length. Square off the ends of each strip, using your set square and cut out. To join strips, take a short end of one strip and place it at right angles on top of a second strip, with right sides together and raw edges level. Machine diagonally across from one corner to the other, forming a slanted seam. Trim away the corner leaving a 6mm (¼ inch) seam allowance and press the turnings open. To finish for bias binding only, press the long raw edges of the strip on to the wrong side so that they meet down the centre (Fig.13).

Piping

Piping consists of a cord covered with a bias fabric strip. It can be inserted into any seam to emphasis the outline of a cover. Ready-made piping is available but it is limited in fabric and colour choice. To make your own, cut a length of piping cord to the length you require

Opposite: Ready-made cords, fringes and tassels add an opulent quality to your covers. Here is a selection of the types found at most large department stores and specialized trimming shops.

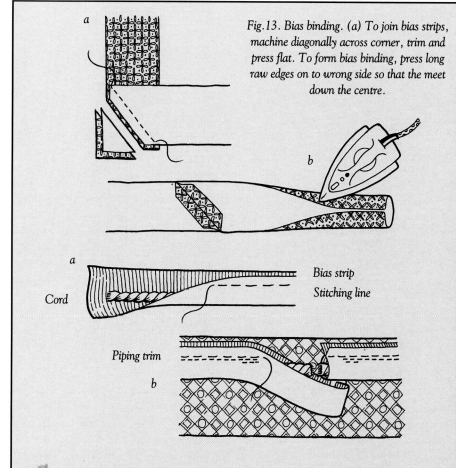

Fig.13. Bias binding. (a) To join bias strips, machine diagonally across corner, trim and press flat. To form bias binding, press long raw edges on to wrong side so that the meet down the centre.

Fig.14. Piping. (a) To cover cord, place it centrally on the wrong side of bias strip, and wrap fabric around. Stitch close to the cord using zipper foot on your machine. (b)To join piping ends, unpick a few stitches on the piping at the finishing end, fold the fabric back and trim cords to butt up. Fold the bias strip back covering the start of the cord, and turn the raw edge under. Stitch in place.

and then make a bias strip (above) that is slightly longer. The width of your strip should be the circumference of your cord, plus a double seam allowance. Join any strips as shown for the bias binding (above). To cover the cord, place it centrally on the wrong side of the bias strip and wrap the fabric around. With raw edges level, pin and stitch close to the cord with the zipper foot on your machine (Fig. 14a).

How to inserting piping into a seam

Place the piping on the right side of one piece of your fabric with the raw edges level. Pin, tack (baste) and machine the piping in place using the zipper foot on your machine, following the row of stitching on the piping and sewing through all three layers. If any corners or curves need to be worked, refer to page 37.

When piping has to be sewn all the way around an item, as on a cushion, start to sew your piping 9mm (⅜ inch) in from the end of the piping strip and finish 5cm (2 inches) from the other end. Unpick a few stitches on the piping fabric strip at the finishing end and fold it back. Trim the cord so that the ends butt together. Fold the fabric back over, covering the beginning of the cord and turning the raw edge under 6mm (¼ inch) (Fig.14b); stitch in place. Complete your seam as normal (p.32) using the zipper foot on your machine.

Gathered frills

Frills add a soft touch to the edges of covers. They can be made of single- or double-thickness fabric and their edges can be trimmed with binding or piping. For a really extravagant look, two frills of different depths can be applied to the same edge. The fullness of a frill depends on the effect you require – it can be anything from one and a half to three times the length of the edge to which it is going to be sewn. The depth of a frill is also dependant on the desired effect; it may be a

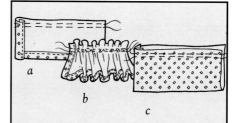

Fig.15. Gathered frills. (a) Single frill – neaten raw edges with double turned hems and work two gathering rows along the raw edge. (b) Pull up gathers to size. (c) Double frill – neaten short ends with a seam, turn to right side and press. Work two gathering rows through both layers along the raw edges.

tiny ruffle around the edge of a throw or a floor length skirt attached to a squab cushion or fitted cloth.

Single frill

Cut your frill to the depth you require, adding a seam allowance to all sides. Seam (p.32) your strips together to obtain the required length. Stitch a 6mm (¼ inch) double turned hem (p.33) along one long edge of the frill – and both short ends if your frill is not being applied in a circle. Work two rows of gathering stitches by hand (p.31) or using your machine, along the raw edge (Fig.15a) and pull up to size (Fig.15b). For long frills, divide the raw edge into sections with pins and gather each section individually to fit the sides of your cover. With the raw edges level, tack (baste) the frill to the right side of your cover and machine in place. Complete your seam as normal (p.32). If the frill is sewn around a hem edge, neaten the turnings and press them towards the cover.

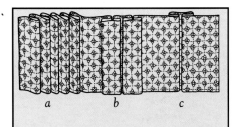

Fig.16. Pleated frills. (a) knife pleats.
(b) box pleats. (c) inverted pleat. Make
sure your pleats are equal in size for a
professional look.

Double frill

A double frill does not need to be hemmed as it has a folded outer edge but, if your frill is not circular, you will need to neaten its short ends. Cut your frill twice the required depth, adding a seam allowance to all sides, and seam the fabric strips together where necessary to obtain the required length. With the raw edges level and wrong sides of fabric together, fold the strip in half lengthways and press. To neaten the short ends, re-fold the strip along the press line, with the right sides of the fabric together and seam across the ends. Turn to the right side and press. Working with both layers of fabric as one, gather (Fig.15c) and attach as shown for the single frill (above).

Pleated frills

As an alternative to gathering, frills can be pleated. There are basically three types of pleats: knife, where they lay in the same direction (Fig.16a), box where two pleats face away from one another (Fig.16b), and inverted, where two pleats face each other (see Fig.16c). When calculating your frill length, allow three times the finished pleat width for each pleat (this is the part of the pleat that is visible from the right side when it is stitched in place). Make up your frill as shown for the gathered type (above) omitting the gathering row. Fold the pleats, keeping them uniform in size, then pin and tack (baste) them in position and apply the frill to your cover as above.

Borders

A border adds a smart, simple edge to a cover. On cushions they can be cut in one with the cover but for pillowcases or duvet covers it is easier to attach a separate fabric strip. Cut out and make a 5cm (2 inches) finished-depth strip, as shown for the gathered frill (above). Sew it flat to the straight sides of your cover, pleating or gathering it to turn the corners (Fig.17b).

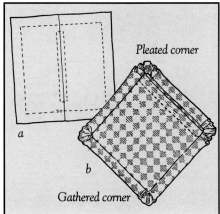

Pleated corner

Gathered corner

Fig.17. Borders. (a) These can be cut in one, on a cover made by the zipped method. (b) A separate strip needs to be inserted for a border on pillowcases or duvet covers. Pleat or gather the strip to go around the corners.

For the all-in-one border, draw your pattern as shown for the basic square or round cushion cover (p.22), but add 5cm (2 inches) to the outer edges for your border. Make up your cover following the basic square or round zipped method, then measure in your border depth from the outer edges and mark the position with a tacking (basting) row. This inner edge of your border can be sewn in place with a row of straight stitch machining (Fig.17a), or, for a more decorative effect, you can work contrasting coloured rows of very close zigzag stitching.

Scalloped edges

This pretty edging can be used to finish the sides of table cloths, throws or bordered cushions. It is best to make a paper pattern for your scalloped shapes, as it is crucial to keep them all the same size and depth. To help you to draw the pattern, use a round object such as a cup or saucer, depending on the size you want for each scallop. Add a seam allowance to the shaped edge, and cut out your pattern. When working on single fabric, for example a table cloth, place your pattern up to the edge and trace around the shape. Trim away the fabric and neaten the edge with a close zigzag machine stitch (Fig.18a).

On a double-thickness cover, the edges need to be shaped before they are seamed together. Lay the pattern up to the edge on your top or front cover and trace and trim the shape as before. Place the shaped cover on top of the base or back cover, with right sides facing. Seam (p.32) the two pieces together around the shaped edge, then trim away the back cover to match the front (Fig.18b).

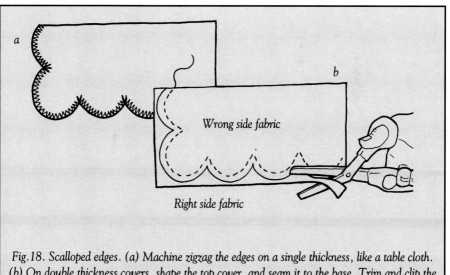

a

b

Wrong side fabric

Right side fabric

Fig.18. Scalloped edges. (a) Machine zigzag the edges on a single thickness, like a table cloth. (b) On double thickness covers, shape the top cover, and seam it to the base. Trim and clip the seam allowances, before turning through to the right side.

READY MADE EDGINGS

Fringes, cords and tassels

Most department stores and sewing specialists offer a wide range of trims, from simple straight fringes to ornate tassels and thick luxurious cords. Fringes are attached to a tape or braid heading that can be hand-sewn to the finished edge of your cover, or hidden by inserting it into a seam during construction.

Some cords come ready mounted on a tape, making them easy to sew into a seam following the piping method (p.39), but cords with no mount need to be hand-sewn to the finished outer edges of your cover. It is a good idea to wrap sticky tape around your cord before you cut it to stop it from unwinding. If you need to join the ends of your cord, unwrap a little at each end and wind them around each other, then tuck the raw ends down into a seam and hand-stitch them together.

Tassels usually have a loop attached to the top which can be inserted into a seam or hand-stitched to the cover. Tassels look great dangling at the end of bolster cushions.

Lace

Lace invokes an image of femininity but while some lace is very delicate and dainty others, such as broiderie Anglaise and heavy crochet lace, can add a wonderfully fresh appeal. No matter which style of edging lace you choose, it will probably have one fancy scalloped edge and the second edge will either be finished or left raw. Lace with an unfinished edge needs to be inserted into a seam where it can be gathered like a frill or applied flat like the strip border. If it has two finished edges, it can be top-stitched onto the right side of a hem, or hand-sewn around a finished cover.

SURFACE DECORATION

Many of the decorative ideas discussed below are crafts in their own right. I am able only briefly to touch on each subject but, if you are inspired to find out more, there are other books in this Country Craft series that deal in more detail with the individual techniques.

Some of the more delicate forms of surface decoration are suitable only for scatter cushions. Think about the end use of your item before you spend a lot of time working on your design. Surface decorations should be applied to your cut pieces, before you begin to sew.

Ribbon and braid

Ribbons and braids can be sewn flat to the surface of a cover, forming a decorative pattern. The simplest way to use ribbon is to tie it into bows and then attach these to your finished cover.

Appliqué

If your machine can do zigzag stitch, then it is easy to appliqué beautiful motifs on to your covers.

Patchwork

Covers made from a mixture of different fabrics have a rustic, old-world charm. This effect is not difficult to create; the secret of a good patchwork is accuracy, both in cutting out and making up.

Quilting

The addition of an extra padded layer, decoratively stitched in place, adds a warm, comfortable texture to the surface of your covers. The quilting stitch can be used in a number of ways, from very basic grid patterns to more ambitious and intricate motifs.

Needlework

Needlework is an increasingly popular pastime and covers are an excellent way for

Above: Here a square cushion has been coordinated with a bolster, by the use of a beautiful fringed trim, mitred at the corners. The bolster itself has been made by adapting the gathered end method, so that the ends are seamed on as separate pieces allowing for piping to be inserted.

you to display beautifully-stitched pieces of work. Tapestry designs are usually worked in thicker yarns on a canvas background and the whole canvas area is filled with stitches, creating a rich, opulent effect. A much daintier style can be achieved with embroidery, which is worked in finer threads, leaving part of the background fabric exposed.

Other ideas

Here are just a few more suggestions for you to think about: pin tucks, crochet, bead work, buttoning, badges, antique treasures and tie-and-dye and fabric paint effects.

BEGINNER'S PROJECT

NOW YOU are ready to start work. As a first project, you are going to transform a basic, everyday chair into something really special.

General Notes

Depending on the style of chair you wish to cover, the pattern pieces may differ slightly in shape and size from the example shown.

A 15mm (⅝ inch) seam allowance is used throughout these instructions and seams are stitched with right sides together unless otherwise stated.

It is best to draw out your pattern pieces and make a cutting plan before you cut into your fabric. This will help you decide where the fabric design needs to be matched or a large motif placed.

MATERIALS

- Main fabric and contrast fabric (for quantities: see instructions below for making the patterns and cutting out)
- Sewing thread to match main fabric

METHOD

To Make Patterns

Take the chair's measurements as shown (Fig.19) and draw out the pattern pieces using the shapes as a guide. Add a 15mm (⅝ inch) seam allowance to all edges of each pattern.

Draw an oblong tie pattern 6cm x 50cm (2½ x 20 inches).

To Cut Out

From the main fabric, cut one seat, two outer backs, one inner back, one front skirt and two side skirts.

From the contrast fabric, cut one back pleat panel, two front pleat panels and two ties.

To Make Up

1. With the top and hem edges level, seam (p.32) a front pleat panel between one side edge of the front skirt and one side edge of a side skirt. Repeat with remaining side edge of the front skirt, the second side skirt and front pleat panel.

2. Fold the joined skirt along each seam with the wrong sides together; press.

3. Working from the right side, fold the front pleat panels to form an inverted pleat (p. 40) each side of the front skirt. The pressed seams should butt together down the centre of each pleat, covering the pleat panels. Pin, tack (baste) and press in place.

4. With the raw edges level, seam the top edge of the joined skirts to the front and side edges of the seat. Match a pleat to each front corner and start and finish your stitching 15mm (⅝ inch) from the back

Opposite: The smooth modern look of this chair cover has been given extra style with the use of contrast fabric for the inverted pleats at the front legs.

Inset: A deep centre back pleat makes it easier to dress your chair, as it allows the cover to slip loosely over the top. It is then held together by ties to create a stylish back detail.

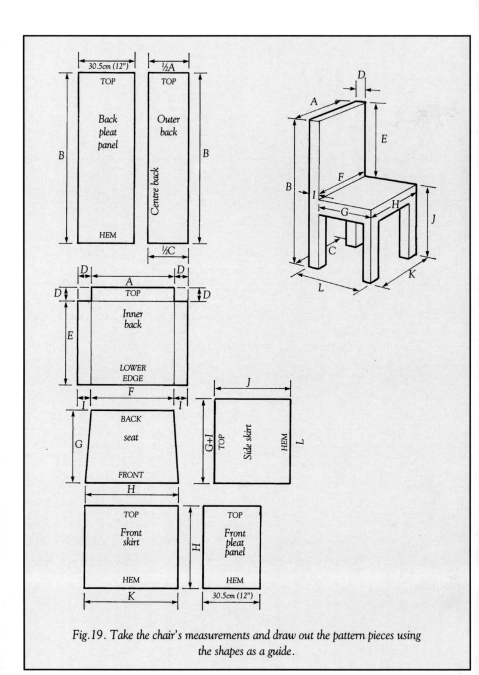

Fig.19. *Take the chair's measurements and draw out the pattern pieces using the shapes as a guide.*

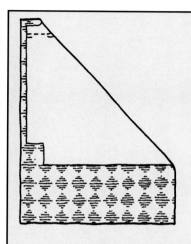

Fig.20. Fold the top edge of the inner back over to one side edge and seam the short top edges together.

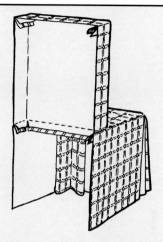

Fig.21. Seam the lower edge of the inner back to the back edge of the seat and extended top edges of the side skirts.

edge of the seat. The ends of the side skirts should extend an equal amount past the back edge of the seat piece.

5. Fold the top edge of the inner back over to one side edge. With the raw edges level, seam (p.32) the short top edges together (Fig.20). Fold the top edge over to the opposite side edge and repeat.

6. Seam the lower edge of the inner back to the back edge of the seat, starting and finishing at the extended top edges of the side skirts (Fig.21).

7. Make up the ties following the narrow tie method (p.35). With the raw edges level, tack (baste) a tie to the right side of one outer back, placing it halfway along the centre back edge. Repeat with the remaining tie and the outer back piece.

8. Seam the back pleat panel between the centre back edges of the outer backs,

sandwiching the ties in place at the same time. Fold and tack (baste) the pleat following steps 2 and 3.

9. Keeping the hem edges level, seam (p.32) the top and side edges of the joined outer backs to the remaining top and side edges of the side skirts and inner back.

10. To finish stitch a 15mm (⅝ inch) single turned hem (p.33) around the hem edges, then slip stitch(p.31) the centre back pleat edges together for 7.5cm (3 inches) from the top edge.

Further Suggestions

For extra comfort, have a foam block (p.14) cut to fit your seat shape before you start, then take all the measurements for your pattern pieces with the foam in place.

You can also define the edges of your cover with contrast piping set into the seat and outer back seams (p.37).

INDEX